THE DEAD TREE GARDEN

THE DEAD TREE GARDEN

poems

Lisa M. Dougherty

NINE MILE BOOKS ❋ SYRACUSE, NEW YORK ❋ 2025

NINE MILE BOOKS
PROPEL DISABILITY POETRY SERIES

Publisher: Nine Mile Art Corp.
Editors: Stephen Kuusisto, Andrea Scarpino

Cover Art: Justin Hamm
Typeset and designed by Philip Memmer

ISBN-13: 979-8-9925462-3-1

Nine Mile Books is an imprint of Nine Mile Art Corp. Publication of this book is made possible by the Propel Foundation. The publishers also acknowledge support from the following entities: the New York State Council on the Arts, the Governor and the New York State Legislature, and the County of Onondaga and CNY Arts through the Tier Three Project Support Grant Program. This publication would not have been possible without these groups. We are grateful to them all.

Nine Mile Books
27 Erregger Terrace, Syracuse, NY 13224

Table of Contents

Forward

Lisa M. Dougherty's *The Dead Tree Garden* is a poetry collection "unlike" many a book, a distinction in this case as I'm talking about originality and something more, a kind of ingenuity. I think of Baudelaire: "It always seems to me that I should be happy anywhere but where I am, and this question of moving is one that I am eternally discussing with my soul." In poetry the soul is a synonym for the reliquary. We position the furniture of our suffering in the soul's room. But Dougherty's poems insist there is life outside containment.

In her poem "Killdeer" she writes:

> Why the sight of thought
> Makes you stand perfectly
> Still in the presence of her
> Absence. You attach yourself to
> Who takes you away from
> The being that you are. Bird
> Is it that you have forgotten
> The cracked shell your heart is
> Nests in the brittle shrubbery
> Of the past growing more
> Present, that you cannot even
> Drag your unbroken wing
> As if it had been
> Brave to desire this
> One transitory body.

It's the "transitory body" we're concerned with, the body we sense fleetingly and which we must must invariably compare to our own. In the hands of a striking poet this comparison is urgent, tender, and sometimes dark. Consider "The Deep Falling Inside Her":

Inside her there is a streetlamp

that some nights she can meet you under
not so far from the pain

as she would have you think,
she pulls you into her

do not flicker through   the deep falling

inside her is a light
you haven't before reached.

The space we feel in these poems would be hard to paint. This has always seemed to me to be one of the great virtues of poetry, that it can center for us things that can't be seen. But feeling enters into these spaces. It often suggests the imagination has come from some great distance. There is a fierce independence to Dougherty's work. Again, consider "Somewhere on the Ledge of Fallen Things":

Somewhere on the Ledge of Fallen Things

Maybe it's a dust covered windowsill. A mantle often overlooked. Or a shelf in the bedroom of your grown child where her most favorite toys have sat long since having been played with. Did you not expect to end up here? At some point, waiting to be picked back up? I suppose you need me to tell you—you can't be all broken. Not all at once anyway. Look here, a glass bottle with a chipped lip. You don't really know why you kept it, but for how the sun still finds a way to pass its light on through. Is that nothing like you? Even the old dried out remains of what used to be a blow flower, left for years between a closed window and an open screen. It still remembers the soft breath of your child lifting its seed. And how she laughed when they all blew back and stuck their fluff in her hair. Are you laughing now? Maybe there's still something here that can help you. Somewhere on the ledge of fallen things, an old wooden earring box your mother had your brother give to you on your seventh birthday. Its hinges nearly pried off from overuse. Or not? But anyway, have you opened its lid lately? If you found its lost song, could you sing it for me?—or just once, try?

As an editor I'm reminded of the work of Tomas Transtromer: "maybe there's something here than can help you" is a splendid address to the reader. Transtromer says "you can see beauty if you look to the side." We want to see the essences but they're not necessarily in front of us. We will, if we're lucky, return to the reliquary described above. These are poems of indelible originality.

Stephen Kuusisto
Editor, Propel Poetry Series

THE DEAD TREE GARDEN

Small as Hope in the Helicopter Rain

Among the tall grass and clover flowers our youngest sits picking. She squints an eye shut and holds one up to the light twisting at its stem. Slow and careful. She wants to know how the sunlight breaks through its petals and so begins pulling them out one by one. Her sing-song voice counting them until they are all gone. What she takes from this she will tell no one. Then a helicopter seed. And a new question as she continues to pick it up and toss it into the air. Despite its falling back to the ground, every time. But soon they are falling all around her. A strong wind has brought them almost fluttering in a way she seems somehow familiar with. And suddenly she is spinning with them. She, this girl we worried so much about her walking late. Always tripping over nothing, and even now still unable to come down off her toes. And yet she is spinning and stretching her arms out as if to welcome something back. Something we at some point lost. Something, small as hope in the helicopter rain.

Autism on the Earth's Delicate Carpet

She tilts her head to one shoulder
And covers her other ear
To write, the sound of a pencil
Is like scratching paper.
And the meltdown
Should she have to erase
More homework than usual tonight.
So I let her take a break out back,
With the condition of bare feet.
And she just lays in the shaded grass
With her shirt lifted over her belly
To feel the coolness
Of the earth's delicate carpet.
At least today she is not in a pace'
Walking the house with her animal
And bumping it into her head.
There is air spray in every room
In case a bad smell.
Because she knows me making
Her favorite muffins
When I'm still mixing in the bowl.
So please don't let them sit her
Next to the kid who farts a lot in class.
She will be honest and extreme!
And yet she tells me things
Like did I know, butterflies
Have taste-buds on their feet?
Or will ask me in a bath how
The tub is liquid with water

That is really two gasses? And why
Doesn't blowing air bubbles change it?
She dries off and gets ready for bed,
Cuddles up shirtless by the air vent
Then puts her feet under the bed
To fall asleep on the floor.
It's her world of small spaces
Her feelings of safeness.
And I get to keep these small moments of her,
When beyond all her questionings
She turns on her music
And we say our *I Love You's*,
It's always, *Can you lay with me?*
And then I just listen to her,
Sometimes still chatting away,
Or, just breathing.

Killdeer

Why the sight of thought
Makes you stand perfectly
Still in the presence of her
Absence. You attach yourself to
Who takes you away from
The being that you are. Bird
Is it that you have forgotten
The cracked shell your heart is
Nests in the brittle shrubbery
Of the past growing more
Present, that you cannot even
Drag your unbroken wing
As if it had been
Brave to desire this
One transitory body.

Less Like Strides Toward Anything

> *Lovers don't finally meet somewhere.*
> *They're in each other all along.*
>
> —Rumi

On a day I couldn't possibly remember,
with the first steps I ever took, I have to imagine
there was a window I was looking out,
but probably stumbled first over some toy,
banged my knee and got distracted.
And you, already seventeen years on your own
time, didn't even notice, but ran too fast
into the tree limb you forgot to duck.
And somewhere along the way as I walked
into my first school, where I didn't smile
and refused a retake for the yearbook,
maybe you were getting ready for your first shift
in a factory where the dogs guard,
and snarling at the gate, chase away
even the slightest scent of happy
you might have hidden not deep enough
in your pocket. You hang on to a quarter
circa the year I was born, and don't know
why you decide to break the bill from your wallet
to cover the twelve odd cents
hung over on your tab at the diner.
How the years were fast by. Seemingly less
like strides towards anything,
and certainly nothing of certainty.
As when I bought my first prom dress
a size too big for me, and you
nervously slid on your first lover's finger,

a ring that didn't fit. And so what?
Is it not a big deal, how small things never are?
          —how I, even with the first shufflings
of my small feet, and you were already so far ahead,
towards the window of all things "We,"
began walking.

The Deep Falling Inside Her

Inside her there is a streetlamp

that some nights she can meet you under
not so far from the pain

as she would have you think,
she pulls you into her

do not flicker through   the deep falling

inside her is a light
you haven't before reached.

You Want an Encore

Where the lips are silent, the heart has a hundred tongues.
—Rumi

our mouths still in silence applaud
for what we both lean quiet into
and so our eyes become a tangled way
my tongue could only twist around with
the taste of you still in my mouth
and the words of after sex fast pulsing
in those unable to speak moments
I'm thinking and I just shake my head
right then when you ask me what?

A Gesture Too Tired Not to Speak

The wound is the place where the Light enters you.
—Rumi

And what would you have placed there? If I
 opened my hands
to you with the loose cup of my palms held
 together.

Would you be able to recognize the sacrament I was asking? Would you accept my body for what its parchment was telling you? Just read through its wounded landscape and don't ask for words. Then maybe you could understand more, how some are born

a cold light's fragment. How the scarred
 glow
through the hovered smoke of dead incense,
 there is still a way
for what is without body to be held. I'll
 ask again,

do you have much faith in me? Because I have wandered far too long and repented nothing. Opened small spaces for light to fill. But never was able to keep warm long. Do you see now,
 the shards
of my fingertips beginning to break? There is little time, I need to open a new place for you

to let me take you in. I have come far
and together we could both stay warm.

Where Something Was Once Made

In a small town where everything
but the people come and go
how they leaned into one another
was all that mattered
in the abandoned archway
at the factory of shadows.

People You May Know

I want to thank Facebook for informing me
I may in fact know my own brother. And I want to
thank Facebook furthermore for giving me the chance to
"Friend" him. Cuz see, I often forget
how the brother I grew up with,
who would often push me to the ground
or throw me into the ditch on the corner
where we were dropped off
exposing my magenta panties to the children left
on the school bus, their encouragements shouting
through the open windows he looked back to,
how he too was just trying to be *liked.*

I want to thank Facebook for giving me a hand
to extend you. The truth, I could not have soon enough
come to think of: the word *brother*
—as would be defined by our sibling relationship
and the word *friend*—as it could be, defined by you,
are synonyms not like the ones they teach
to my six-year-old daughter in school. How I pray
she will learn this on her own, more quickly than I did.
I want to thank Facebook for a simple button,
and the two small words *+add friend* in a rectangular box,
the ease of sending you a request, by no means small.
And I want to thank Facebook for the button
they will send for you to accept, in its own rectangle
should you tap twice, I could begin again
to "Like" something, anything at all, about you.

How Nothing Ever Rises into Place

There is no uncertainty left for the apples that fall to the ground. Or for the teenage girl whose father shared publicly the video he took of her hair piled on the floor after cutting it off as punishment for a misdeed. What it was she understood as she looked down a few days later when he was done was all she took with her when she jumped from the overpass? There is something to be learned from a baby bird that hesitates before flying. How falling is the only direction we know for sure.

Maybe if I Start Small

If it meant pushing you to safety, I'd like to think
I would have put myself in the path of an oncoming car.
But honestly, I can't be sure. If I would have
been there to punch out the teeth
of the classmate who picked on you
in the lunch line, I would have done so
for no other reason than *No One Fucks with Family.*
"It's just principle" I'd say, though not so plain and simple.
And I admit, it wouldn't have been for the right reasons.
But it still seems strange to think how I was protective
of you, my older brother. Because you are
that feeling like a fist clinched inside my chest
so tightly the nails have permanently pressed
their crescent shapes, side by side onto the heel of my palm.
Perhaps that is why even the want to forgive you
doesn't really surprise me so much
as it angers me that I haven't figured out how.
But maybe if I start small, take your hands for example,
begin by forgiving that one part of you. Then
maybe we could celebrate. For the hand
I would open to you is all ready, decorated
with a banner.

Somewhere on the Ledge of Fallen Things

Maybe it's a dust covered windowsill. A mantle often overlooked. Or a shelf in the bedroom of your grown child where her most favorite toys have sat long since having been played with. Did you not expect to end up here? At some point, waiting to be picked back up? I suppose you need me to tell you—you can't be all broken. Not all at once anyway. Look here, a glass bottle with a chipped lip. You don't really know why you kept it, but for how the sun still finds a way to pass its light on through. Is that nothing like you? Even the old dried out remains of what used to be a blow flower, left for years between a closed window and an open screen. It still remembers the soft breath of your child lifting its seed. And how she laughed when they all blew back and stuck their fluff in her hair. Are you laughing now? Maybe there's still something here that can help you. Somewhere on the ledge of fallen things, an old wooden earring box your mother had your brother give to you on your seventh birthday. Its hinges nearly pried off from overuse. Or not? But anyway, have you opened its lid lately? If you found its lost song, could you sing it for me?—or just once, try?

Someday Her Song Will Fall Silent

> *I want to sing like the birds sing, not worrying about*
> *who hears or what they think.*
>
> —*Rumi*

Five minutes in and she's just getting started.
Her sweet voice dipping into something quieter
when she doesn't know the words. She doesn't care,
when I try to fill in the missing parts
she puts her hands over her ears and continues,
singing it the way I imagine she must hear it.
And, as if tapping out the notes,
she punctuates the air with her fingers
half dancing through the kitchen.
Who knows how long she will go on for
or how many songs she will mangle
and mash together, like taking the wrong turn
on a path that splits. I ask her to stop,
and smile as when she turns it up, I realize
someday her song will fall silent.
Not all at once though, but gradually
it will taper off as she grows,
get lost in her memory somewhere,
or she'll leave it behind one day on her way to
school.
And she won't remember to pick it back up.
So I'll have to go looking for it, in her backpack,
at the bus stop, or somewhere on the
playground
where she might have dropped it
to run off and play with her friends at recess.
I'll search the hallways after hours

and give up having not found
what's not meant for me to find.
Anyway, she'll already have turned away,
as all children do, as we all must have
at some point, leaving behind a silence
more frustrating than all the wrong
words stuck in your head
and songs it seems won't end.

The Simple Way of Her

She holds her right arm above her head in a gentle arc. Her fingers form a pinching gesture, and her wrist turns inward as if she is about to spin a top. In her excitement, she is up on her toes and stumbles forward a bit. She is wearing a new dress and, as with all her new dresses she is testing the twirl. A pirouette. And then another. And another. One after another until she is tired and stops, holding her arms out to the sides of her proclaiming her doneness with a brilliant "Ta-dah!" She is satisfied with the function of her dress. A good twirl will fill the short skirt of it with air and its lift lifts her. Sends her spinning into her own realm of things beautiful. And this is the way of her. The simple and often awkward way of her. And it is why I imagine she refuses to see the ugliness that lies around her. Around all of us. She spins and it all blurs into something streaked with streamers and awe. And it is why I enjoy watching her, and for now try not to think about how as she grows that ugliness will begin to seep in. She will spin and become dizzy with flashes of it as it breaks through. And at some point, she will stop. But for now I try not to think about how she will stop spinning and how she will eventually walk forward and face what we all must face. Her dresses will begin to have a new function. They will tighten around her; their silhouette will form to her body and would no longer lift so easy in the air if she tried them. I try not to think about that. About how and why she will forget to quit trying them. And not ask her what was beautiful she saw in them. For what it is to her is easy. Unnamable but easy. And for now, just remember what is simple. A dress with a good twirl, that lifts her.

My Realistic Eye

I could try to take
a piece of charcoal to paper
or a soft pencil
and draw a realistic eye,
shade the flecks of her iris
and the way her lashes curl,
but her eyes, they change
with every twirl,
and as her dress lifts around her
her head swirls
a new expression towards me,
her eyes are never fixed.
I see in her how everything is
transitory, a momentary blessing
that will change if you look away.
And I try to watch her close
but she moves as if movement can
live in the thought
of what keeps on going
might just catch her for a moment,
still her for a breath.
And so my realistic eye
puts down the pencil or charcoal
and just watches her,
in a way I could never keep.

Somewhere a Place

I wanted to leave
something there for you
to find, the wings of a dragonfly
strung under a small tree
a glint of light against dark bark,
to go there before you,
to mark a trail
with what is small.
Sticks that have grown
less ordinary and curious
as a curl of smoke.
But it is a somewhere
we disappear into
by way of the light
shift of wind
through our held hands.
It is a place
I could not go
without you.

The Strands that Keep Me Together

There are three of them, and they are the strands that keep me together. Two young daughters and an 18yr. old that seems to have so suddenly become man. Still, I can't help remember sitting cross-legged at a coffee table and playing board games and hours of Rummy with him. His quiet voice in him when I picked him up from grade school and ask about his day. How I'd have to roll the windows up and turn the radio down to hear what was in him. Or what was in him then when he said the moon was a broken bowl? And how it was with a fist full of crayons he banged his head under his father's desk that started a melting in him. All that before the two that will rough tumble just to get a piece of him. Pulling at both his arms as if they could stretch him into both their wants. The flash-lit faces they've seen of him. And the hymns I see in them, still glowing.

Alongside

For my daughter Amara and her best friend Kyrah

To school she wears long sleeves
And slips on her knit gloves to avoid
The unwanted feel of paper.
She crawls off her bed
Sleeping by the air vent
Beneath a tent made
Of her comforter, stripped down
To undergarments
Just enough to keep
The feel of a constant
Cool on her exposed skin.
Goes into immediate
Retreat at the mention of a hug,
Climbing her voice
Against the undesired touch.
Stretches her cuffs
Beyond the length of fingertip
To practice formation
With her ice-skating partner.
But she has a friend
On a different end
Of a brilliant spectrum,
Equally radiant with
Both smiles and affirmations,
Her own determination.
So today someone stomps
Another foot
Asserting the hardwood
Echoes in my direction.

Still there's only one name
She has ever
Intentionally recalled. With the way
My memory purposely holds on,
The way with her forgetful
About anything else mind,
She's held on
Almost 5 years now,
To the only one I've ever seen,
With whom she walks alongside,
Nothing getting in between
Them and with what
Their bare hands hold
Together.

Husband

Wonder if you will against what time and never again you thought might erase me. You hear a scratching pencil when my mind is widdling wood. All I have is a pencil tip. It scratches at the paper like nails devouring layers of innocent skin. Tried to make a garden bed tilled at the nape of my neck. What has been planted does not know anything of the soil from which it may grow. My neck. It's been a long time since I have had a ring on a chain there.

Ascribe

A shoe grazes the floor and *scuffs* its way into a language against her. When the flying grass-hopper jumps trying to open its wings against the lid of an emptied Cool Whip container, is then, *desperation* not a sound. Do the ears of an autistic child not multiply into the same factor of what perspective a bee's eye makes into our distortion. What she hears different when a chair is pulled out in the kitchen, she can only name as an assault directly set into wavelength. *Screech*, I imagine was named for the way she'd tear through the seemingly quiet. *Enough*. She waves a white flag with her fingers pressed into the side of her head as her feet *pound* for *pound* her path up the stairs to where she cannot run any further away. And yet, the sky. The same sky she would point her little finger to and draw the *ooh* out of the moon When it sounds as if it could *break* sound. *Asleep*, is a sound, I listen through the cracked door for. The sky, it does not wake her.

She Paces the Halls

The never adagio
Composed fret
Attuned against
Her body's tempo
Metronomely anxious
Silence and heeled
Steps between
The paced house
Acoustic with
Her heavy feet.

Getting Ready

School is starting, the supplies lists
Have been double checked,
Backpacks ready to go, packed
Their lunches on the kitchen counter.
Names on everything
In black Sharpie pen.
They are both in bed early,
We'll rise and send them
Off on different buses.
But for now, it's getting ready
All the paperwork.
And still some to fill out, when
A question I don't even know is
Just the word *Period.*
She's only eight… Not yet.
I still want her to believe in moth dust
And tie a string to her foot
As she tries to flutter away

Ask of the Feather You Found on the Ground

Did you not want to be part
Of what flies? What finds
The current to ride
Effortless through the air?
Ask what you broke
De-fleshing yourself from
The natural pattern, of something
For you. I pour another glass
In the birdbath of ice and whisky.
Bathe long after the sun
Feathers the sky the color of after-birth.
And you think because you are the gray
Too often gazed on by, that maybe
You are not something uniquely taken,
Flighted from the path of a spectrum
Not quite defined. Ask if it is not
Something, that you've been
Thrown off of,
The balance this left
Wing
Has relied on.

Matins for Dziadzia

The clawed chest
I sometimes wake up to,
The scapular you were
Never dressed without.
And the crooked grin
Behind the bend of your
You've been naughty finger.
I can still hear
The disapproval you never
Spoke. A sacrament I thought
Worth breaking, the scissors
And urn necklace stolen
From the funeral home.
I'm sure you saw
I cut your hair. So,
It was smoke.
The wispy gray curl
Of what you had left,
The smell of church
And lighting the round disk
Of coal to serve a funeral,
Waiting for the dead
Incense to fill my lungs.
Pretending it was the fire
That brought me here.

Accolades Against Being Forgotten

Words like *Oplatek*,
The sometimes glimpse back
Of outstretched hands
Holding pink and white wafers.
The un-still belief.
Believing because of them
We were blessed
As the taste of nothing
Dissolved somewhere between
Aroma-soaked tongues
And bent arms strung like
Popcorn garland around waiting.
Of the young and not yet
Grown of us
Dancing to Polish carols
You took the words to
With you. That year
I ran my hand along
Your spine,
Was the first and last
Time something below your skin
Poked at me.
Jutted the splintered bone
Of awareness, shredding
Through all the times
I held against you
How proud you were
Of the daughter you had raised
With accolades against

Being forgotten. What was
Never known
Words under grown just over
A year later. We knew
The small straw drawn
The day you died was a language
In itself was
The unrecognizable longed for.

She Couldn't Move

For Aunt Leona, died Feb. 1, 2018

But still, there were the holidays.
She didn't let on,
And primped her hair
With volume and color,
Wore festive sweaters
So no one would ask
When she lightly swept down
Our unknowing spines
With her hand asking
How it was
We were, without knowing
How she was keeping
Our faint heart beats
Stronger by the rhythm
Of Christmas Polka
On the boom- box
Where cassette tapes were still
Accepted. The words *Polished*
I may never know
Is the loss of
What was not shared,
The sound
Or the meaning of?

We Planned

But it wasn't natural,
They had to induce.
And she wasn't breach.
She didn't come
Through my vagina
Butt first
With her cord wrapped
Around her neck.
Though her heart rate
Dropped her oxygen levels
Low so she is still now
Six years high on her toes
Twirling every new dress
Like the tresses of hair
That never seem to grow
But rather wrap themselves
As if they were ribbons
Scraped taught by the edge
Of a scissor blade
and let loose.
I remember there was a tub
In the hospital room
As if it would have been a spa
Treatment insurance would have
Paid for the luxury of
A comfortable delivery.
They kept me turning over.
I told you they would

Take her by cutting me open,
Something you didn't want to believe
Until you had to,
And the gurney rolled
To the room with OR lamps
Lit up like bathroom light
First thing on a dark morning.
You saw blood
Opening her way
As I closed my fist
White knuckled around
The IV pole, your voice
Might have saved me.
I don't remember
What you said
Was more a feeling
You can't go away from.
And then she was,
Pulled into this world of ours
With the loud pop
Of a child pulling a sucker
From a mouth
That didn't want to let go.

And Not a Child

Remind me because I have
Longed for the template
Of kindness, this idea
That a door held open
Or a shopping cart offered
At the local grocery
Could matter. More than
A signature inscribed check,
The artificial gesture of
What supports you. Will you
Listen a moment
To what we haven't touched,
Names we haven't called,
On what playground
Do we keep the fingers we have
Pointed toward what
We want to name *other*
As if separation is desire
And not a child
Who does not want
To go to bed at night
Asking to be slept with,
Afraid of morning
And waking up without?

To All Those Whom Prophet False

I un-dear you this. For. I'd have believed you if you said a short lifeline. But in against love, lie. You fed me brevity. When I cannot feel anything that doesn't begin with his hand. Holding everything. Unpredictable. I see the way of every kernel. Taking to its form. Whatever pops from. Within. It. A new secret of it cobbled. Originates. The way of each droplet of rain. Recanting the cold in unprecedent. Shape. Is distinction. Not a way. Of being othered by. And then. What is to say of the nature. To want to. Be. Sometimes the othered. I have offered. To him the contour of my disposition. Asymmetry. Or the idea of. Seeing myself a hologramed attendance. In his palm's opened absence. A psalm against. How I was wanting. To be unwrinkled. As a sheet. Caught straight by the weight of water. Wind dried into what you say. Will die. Do lines not reach further. When. Soldered will hold unsevered. How is our nature. Anything but. Not Together?

You Understood Something Other

As the heart of a Tiffany lamp,
The soldered seems
Of what appears broken, fixable.
How your worked hands
Bent and arthritic
From years of kneading,
Still hoisted a wheelchair
From the back of a station wagon,
Scooped her rigid body
Every morning as she woke
From the bed you built
Of 2x4's and mesh screen,
To keep her safe;
Crushed the Frosted flakes
With the bottom of a cup
So your granddaughter didn't have to chew
Too much. Her teeth were pulp,
And I've had to fish her denture
From a bag of stool.
But still, we would annoyed look at you
When you told us how to do
The smallest detail of every day,
And the weight of a washcloth
With the burden of drool. You lifted
When you heard her voice,
The unintelligible coos.

Revealed

Having to re-educate
Your body every time
A new wheelchair.
And the one we learned
Together the necessity
Of water in a battery,
That Halloween you were
A clown and we joked
As I pushed and pulled
However I could
Up the hill until someone.
Or how I've bathed you
In a different chair
As we tossed fun at the wall
Your palsied fist had to pound
The words out of.
Holding your arms up
To shave you into
What's expected of a woman,
And thinking what a waste
Of perfect bikini-line.
Why I thought
I was brave, when
Soap suds were all
That kept you clothed
And you never had
To see me naked.

Black Orchid

As if a petal could unwilt,
She would grow herself into
A hideous bloom. Layered
With the forgotten palette
Of everything that dies
Without blush.
Dig and you'll find her
Where your fingers stain.
In the damp soil of shadows
You uncover a girl.

Turned to Her

Her arms
Pressed
So brilliantly
To her chest
Is a shield
Against
My back
Turned
To her
Pouring
Her favorite
Chips
In a bowl
So
I can feel
Her armor
Jumping
Up
And down
With an almost
Unfound
Utterance
She says it,
Says she does

Me, unwound
When I know
It's what I'd give
Anything for
To hear
How even
The blue
A plastic bowl
I must forget
As her words
Sound
Clear as when
She brings it
Back empty
Again
She's found
A way
To sway again
Left into
What is
Right
Through me.

The Dead Tree Garden

She is pacing, as she normally does, waiting for the school bus. Today it is outside, the weather being a bit warmer. And suddenly she remembers it is supposed to be spring now. The garden beds are still *barren.* A word I accidentally dropped in conversation and had to explain the meaning of. The bus is still not here. So she begins picking up twigs. Holding them up she notices they are like small replicas of the trees still without leaves. Admires their nakedness. And so she wants to keep them, begins to plant them in the soft soil, chattering and telling me when I try to stop her that, she knows they will not grow. The bus is late again. She is finished and stands up proud of what she has just done. If they don't come soon, I will have to take her in. Avoid off-setting her day should she miss breakfast. She likes to eat with the other kids. But now she is smiling, telling me it is her "Dead Tree Garden." And so it is. And the bus isn't going to get here in time. I run to grab my keys, glance back at her and her garden of dead trees. I don't tell her that the wind will soon blow it down.

Fold

cut here   here cut
this into something   or   something into this
that you are   are you that
slow falling   inside   falling slow
towards something   something towards

Five Years Later

After the doctor
Who finally healed me
But first took one look
Then sent me away
To another that gave up,
And the other three
Had no luck either.
Finally the skin taken
From my leg left
In rectangular scars,
That purple in cold reminder
Of the times we couldn't spend,
Tongues I didn't see stuck
Out in the yard
As the snow fell
In thick flakes
You caught on the tip
Of childhood went
With the years
You'd hold my pinky
As we'd walk to the corner
Store, the warm days
My hand held on to the hand grip
Of the arm crutches
That like a playground
Taunted your small minds
To swing on the edge
Of forbidden things.
To get what I deserved,

How you knew what
I was asking for
When I stepped into boots
As the frozen sky began
To let go, I gathered up
The two balls of snow
That surprised your faces
And the seconds I held
My arms out expecting
The five years you dealt
Me in return.

Taillights

They are just nine and nearly six and we are waiting, or I am, for the school bus. Our oldest tells her sister to dive into the snow. The first snow. White and too shiny for morning eyes. I scold her and tell her to get out. Practical but over reactive. Her pants will get wet. I feel a sadness poke me in the stomach. I am the monster that made her stomp off flakes of her child. The wind is gusting, and the bus motor sounds up the hill. Of course she picked out her magenta fleece pants today. A few quick swipes to make sure the rest won't melt through as the bus squeals to a stop. They race to see who gets on first. Waking up every morning, neither want to go. Every day. "I love you!" and "Have a good day!" as they climb on, the youngest always awkward fumbling her way up the steps, reaching for the rail to pull herself up as her backpack slides and weights her arm down. It's a secret code for PHWEW! Once they're gone. But still. It's way to still. The bus has rounded the corner and passed behind our house. And the sounds begin to fade. Feet hammering through the hallway and up the stairs, re-plays of PJ Masks from the next room over, the oldest constant with "Mom, can I ask you a question?", sink water I know shouldn't be running. Still. I stare at the angel in the snow.

She Talks in Muddy Puddles

Sometimes as the rain falls
Softly into the dips
Of when she used to let us
Hold her up for a picture
Smiling her wayward curls
As she'd press her face
To a cheek's touch.
Something less delicate
A too much pondered child,
Curiously set to motion
But aware of the danger
Of touching a moth's wing.
Or when she let
Her clothes match
As we had walked out
Towards the falling sky,
Before she did not want told
How pretty she was,
Daunting ladybug
Boots and matching parka.
Her mind too busy
Trying to negate things,
Or navigate
As she stomped mud
From the pooled
Miniature wetlands
Between the strips of grass
And the asphalted road.

What she questioned
Was more her,
And the right to ask
Not for a long lecture
Or the answer to,
She was always
Closer than we thought.
As for the questions she asked
I tried to rinse out then,
Only now realizing
It was stiffness
She wanted nothing of,
A stark resolution for her
Would never be stomped out
Where small lakes are
Big enough
Two small feet could find
The bottom fast.
As she skipped
Past all the puddles
Of clear water. Never
Standing still.

Trails of Green Light

So. Today the rain drips narrow through the smoke exhaled from my mouth standing inside the side door of the garage where I ash incessantly flicking my cigarette with the upward and downward strike of my thumb off the wet end of dinged filter. Like a painting drowned in watercolor too watered down. Its rise set for another day as its lift falls an instant blanket toward the spatted ground. Nothing seems to be of flight. Somewhere the moths hide their dusted wings beneath the Hosta leaves umbrellaing a shelter in the garden bed. The bees sleepy in their hives keep to a low hum. So. It is like you to remind me their pollen will be collected from the pistons of lilies for sure when some tomorrow opens the warmth of the kind of sky you'd tilt your head back and close your eyes to see the trails of green light that dart like shooting stars burning out beneath the dark of your lids. It is then the moths will unfold their wings to twirl then zig and maybe a zag or two above the Campanula Bells, you'd say. So. Isn't it like you to disclose another secret. Tucked like the deep breath, something you want to tell me, held gray and swirling rings inside an unlocked chest.

Ask Why We Ask What We Do Not Want

To ask of the shaggy haired man, with the grayed-out straggly tips. Who weights your pockets with more than a passing by? Is there even a half-smile he has made sure not to spend wastefully? What is it that made his fingers seizure a tune I may possibly know? Could it be, we were once sung together? Over a cheeseburger laughing our way through a broken fret. Someone could stop and lend a beat-box. Ask us, or more often you, who fretted then over what to someone else seemed small. Again walking by. Ask again if you do or do not belong to the class of purposefully ignoring. Oh, that's right, you did take in a stray dog. Saw in your mind the puppy playgrounds where it is cool to keep a plastic bag dangling from your pocket. Had in mind that moment where she would run to you. That to her sound attention. To the strum of what you named her. Played off your lips the vibrating of something. Isn't that why he sings? To that having your name called is something song. Ask his name. It just might be that something that would denote what is hopeful or fierce, or both.

Ask Me to Light

A charcoal disc
The warm edge glow
Ask me not to
Somehow like this
Sizzling of incense
Ask my eyes not to light
With the intensity
Of a child at bat
The licking of lips
The tightening grip
Gum wadded in cheek
Flavored spit swallowed
What will become of ash
We didn't ask
Told we will return to
Someone's nostrils flare
In the scent deadened
With perfumed blessing
It wasn't the smoke
So ask why
Or what it was
Other than dirt
In your eye
Kicked up
That made you miss
Swinging towards
The almost fire.

Ask of the Bone that Splinters

When broken upon
With the feverous
Half snapped,
Ask of the bones'
Willed splintering
How the galaxy
Of a dog's tongue
Begins to observe
What might be
Explored
When you prefer
A tooth instead,
To puncture into
Release
The flavor of exposition
Only he can extract
The particular atmosphere
Of the desired
One you allow space
To conceal a wish
Among the sharded
Guard, the sought after
Taste of your marrow.

Can I Tell You Now

Because I knew
With the low hum
Of everything she couldn't say
You'd go sleepy eyed
Into coo with that call
No body wanted
To help you make,
It was your way
Onto the cold silver
Slapped with what was
When I saw
The coiled chord
As the IV line stretched
And when the buttons were dialed
Is what was
When I walked out.

Something Other than Nuzzle

The Blue Jays have nested
In the tree beside the garage,
Where two jay-lings hop
With downed wings
Still fuzzed and just
Beginning to feather.
Their bodies effort
To become simultaneously
Alternate ends of a slinky
Around its circled
Ring of scattered bark.
When they stop
And their beaks touch
It is something
Other than nuzzle.
They are waiting to be fed,
And might startle to notice
I am too close. I think
Of you, as in a squawk
I can almost hear
The height of your pitch
As you'd whisper a titter,
As mother bird locks on,
Bobs into the hungry
Neck, cocks a violent rocking
Chirp, as if you were here,
As if I wasn't watching,
Taking in everything
You fed me.

The Deer Come to Eat

Summer is coming back
And you are still
Spearmint leaves
In the garden, small and wild
With weeds and things
You didn't need
To be pulled.
How I didn't understand
The way of your eyes
With those early strawberries
That we couldn't help
But watch the deer bend to eat.
And your jumping
To tap us to notice
The windows behind where
Hummingbirds came to feed.
Or the way then was
Never mattered until now,
Is why your hands tended
To everything
But what, I never asked.

Scapular Un-Hung on My Daughter's Neck

How never I thought
More of what thin plastic
Sheathed the Holly
Remembrance
To the sweated skin
Of your back
As you labored above dough
In a bakery before hours
Your children didn't even know,
Was so close to what
Would translate to the sharp
Knife, that cut behind
What is better left
Not to know, or to see
How what she has
Grown slowly into
Is the neck
I know not
To hang
Your life on.

How Far Is Introvert Willing

To
Dive
Farther
Down
When
Each
Individual
Thrust
Becomes
That
Much
Further
In

Tell Me Again

I should have
Been there.
Cutting up pancakes,
Feeding you time
While monkeys
Hung from ropes.
I should have listened to you.
So tell me again,
With your crooked finger, point
The paths they swung
From one ceiling tile
To another. You,
As drugged laughter begins
To slip.
Tell me again,
What did you make
With your knotted hands?
How many loaves
Of thoughts kneaded
Were delivered
In silence at 4 a.m.?
I want to talk.
To all the secrets,
However many
People ate.

Tell Me Something of the Silences You Heard

As the alarm clock rang
Waking to another shift
Of 4am late nights
Or early mornings
Where your hands meditated
Over mixtures of flour
Salt and yeast kneaded
Silence, and you heard
Drill sergeants preparing,
The wings of hummingbirds
Flapping, shots fired
At targets that would bleed
More than the sound
Of torn paper,
Or paper cut perfectly
For wrapping a present.
Tell me when you pressed
The dough, maybe you felt
A silence of something
That matters.
Something matted
With the thought
Someday
One wants to still
Climb
On your shoulder,
Up the ladder
Of tell me,

Ring out the truths
Your hands must have
Knuckled over.
Tell me why this wasn't
Worth listening to
At the time. Too young
I guess to imagine
There would ever be
A point to that
Crooked finger,
To the simplicity
Of a squirrel
And its cautious gaze.
How you'd laugh
Toward pained glass
As it fed from a feeder
Meant for birds,
And you chirped.

Saw Again the Infamous Owl

Swooped then, just as before. In the crossroad of what my teenager knew as Ghost Lane. A place we partied down the road, amongst the tombstones found in the abandoned creek. It was there it lent its careless glide so close I could see nothing but *It* in front of my side of the windshield. So close I heard its talons ask a pane of glass to become not something between us. And so it didn't. As the tires chirped a quick "Oh Shit," it paused its flight. Lifted itself backward and spanned its wings, as if I weren't already impressed. Then thrust their might forward, climbing backward up a downward escalator, it pothered neither forward nor backward. And then, maybe I was just to overcome, maybe from the glint of amber. Eyes too often not hesitated for. Or was I too overwhelmed? Could he see the sun's white glare off my tightened grip. Have we both seen the same difference?

Something Arbitrary that Had to Do With Chaos

Maybe it was when we pulled into the drive. Saw the streetlights, apparently on sensors had already turned on. And you were. With eyes in the dim. Orange glow of fog lights from the harbor's light house, or maybe gymnasium lights when you first walk into a basketball game. Most would say it's something to get used to. Others a warning, brought on early by the impending storm. When dark fell, we gazed excited. The smell of heavy damp, dirt weighing down wind. I wanted to curl my hand against your cheek as if to cup the crest of a wave. Slow the fall of shadow on your sideways grin. So it could have been the fear of drowning too fast when I could no longer define the edges of your face gone to the soft dark. Or maybe I saw the way I'd let you. Dribble me into a quick switch. Leaving always in the direction I step away from.

Look

The sky is a mother,
A father, everything Grand,
An Aunt you didn't know
You'd miss Uncle,
A sibling you'd riot,
Something so Pontius
Pilot your eyes
Toward a
Backwards. What
You didn't say, how
You could have acted,
What you should have done
Didn't. The sky.
Look back,
Do you not think
One day it will wear
Your name?

The Wind Has a Name It Tells No One

The wind has a name it tells no one. It believes in nothing common. Only slightly whispers of something you think you might recognize. Something more often hidden like the tucked wing of a *coccinellidae,* or if the wind speaks Latin, scarlet. Or the unseen slime left in the trail of a snail. The tomato worm you can't find chewing your garden into what stalks you. As your eyes search. An end to this frustration. Something it wants to tell you but knows better. And so you guess. As the blue swallowtail sets it feet against thirst in another pool of nectar. As the night-crawler tries to make its way back to dirt as the sidewalk begins to dry. You smoke your cigarette. Take your time to think. Try any language you like. Ask as many questions you can. The wind, it will never tell.

Acknowledgments

Some of the poems in this collection appeared in *Congeries, Gargoyle, Lake Effect, Nixes Mate, Redactions, Trailer Park Quarterly,* and in the anthologies *Alongside we Travel: Contemporary Poets on Autism* (NYQ Books 2019), *Keystone Poetry: Contemporary Poets on Pennsylvania* (Pennsylvania State University Press 2025).

Poems also appeared in the chapbook *Small as Hope in the Helicopter Rain* (Cervena Barva Press), and in the chapbook *The Answer is Not Here* (2019 NightBallet Press) coauthored with Sean Thomas Dougherty.

About the Author

Lisa M. Dougherty is the author of the chapbook *Small as Hope in the Helicopter Rain* (Cervena Barva Press) and coauthor of the chapbook *The Answer is Not Here* (2019 NightBallet Press). Her work has appeared in the anthologies *Alongside we Travel: Contemporary Poets on Autism* (NYQ Books 2019), *Double Kiss: Stories, Poems, Essays on the Art of Billiards* (Mammoth Books 2017), and *Keystone Poetry: Contemporary Poets on Pennsylvania* (Pennsylvania State University Press 2025). Her poem "Kildeer" was short-listed for the Pushcart Prize. She lives in Erie, PA with her husband and their two daughters.

A disabled poet who has battled long-term illness for much of her adult life, Dougherty writes, "I was born and raised in Erie, Pennsylvania. As a disabled person who is both cared for and cares for other disabled people, place for me is often an intimate concept as it extends no further than the bus stop where my daughters, particularly my autistic daughter, wait to go to school, or a doorway where I pause to smoke or stare at the backyard, unable to leave the house that day due to pain. Or the places I narrate of my grandfather and his dementia, before his passing, or my cousin with Cerebral Palsy who I helped care for growing up. I hope these poems speak to you well of this intimate world and the lyric sense of place I fight to make for me and my family up here in the far corner of Pennsylvania."

More Titles from the Propel Disability Poetry Book Series

The Importance of Being Feeble-Minded by Nathan Spoon

How Can I Say It Was Not Enough? by Anne Kaier

Swoon by D. J. Savarese

Inside the Invisible by Daniel Simpson

Creating the Faces and Other Poems by Tito Rajarshi Mukopadhyay